How to Hug

and Other Poems

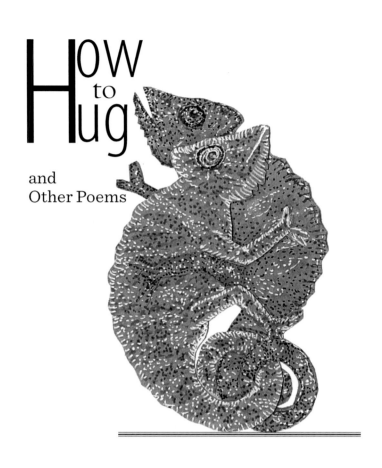

Susie Maguire

MARISCAT
PRESS 2009

ISBN 978 0 946588 51 0

Acknowledgements

'The Hero' was published in the Scottish PEN online magazine and 'Song of the Siren' in *Deliberately Thirsty* 5.

Cover illustration by Susie Maguire

Typesetting and design by Gerry Cambridge
www.gerrycambridge.com
Set in Sentinel Book and Myriad Pro

Printed by Clydeside Press, 37 High Street, Glasgow G1 1LX
clydesidepress@btconnect.com

Published by Mariscat Press, 10 Bell Place, Edinburgh EH3 5HT
hamish.whyte@btinternet.com

Contents

For my Poetry Parents

The Artist's Prayer for his Parents

For those long dry years in the wilderness
For the sudden-tilting landscapes to explore
For language barriers, the need for camouflage
For depriving me of vital human contact
For remaining impervious to my mental distress
For pushing me into dangerous places
For providing me with reasons to be fearful
For appointing me the clan scapegoat
For hobbling my ambitions with doubt
For imbuing me with suffocating guilt
For asking me to wait, to put myself last
For suggesting things could only get worse
For teaching me to be foremost a dutiful child
For making me play with others I mistrusted
For keeping me ignorant of my own needs
For ensuring I took no affections for granted
For telling me I would never be understood —
For these and other transgressions, I thank you,
From the bottom of my abyss, I thank you,
From the peak of every mountain scaled, I thank you,
For each rare gleam of inspiration, I thank you,
For ever and ever-after, always slightly angry, always rather afraid,
In nomine patris et matris, et spiriti sancti, amen.

Breaking up with the Imaginary Boyfriend

It's over. Yes, it was good, at times, in an
odd way, but I need to move on. Besides,
I never really got to know your face —
you shimmered just out of focus, tall,
dark, confidently handsome, gaze always
averted, so that I kept looking, waiting
for you to turn round and pay attention.
Why did I put you up there, on that silly
pedestal?
          Well, your rival materialised
at last. He's not tall, more like my height,
doesn't have your heroic hair or chiselled jaw,
but smiles a lot, and knows what ears are for.
You're disappointed, I understand, I really do —
but I've come to see I need the kind of boyfriend
who (even if he's imaginary too) prefers holding
hands to deconstructing Houellebecq.

Clever Girl

You 'like' Rebecca, you say. You're with her because
'I never have to tell her anything more than once.'
So important to you, that trait, to know she'll process
The vital knowledge you dispense, Gurdjieff-style,
With all the personality of an Intel chip — to view her
As your rather clever pupil. In another universe
Perhaps there's another you, a kinder guru who enjoys
The company of mortals, their not infrequent crashes,
Their clumsy, sticky keys, their random access memories.

Dear Mr Winnicot

'If the artist (in whatever medium) is searching for the self, then it can be said that in all probability there is already some failure for that artist in the field of general creative living. The finished creation never heals the underlying lack of sense of self.'

—D.W. Winnicot, psychologist (1968)

Hello, dear Mr Winnicot (D.W., if I may) — and
Thank you for that clever little nutshell; your
Wise kernel most gratefully received, sniffed at,
Sucked, and tucked in cheek-pouch for later
Gnawing/indigestion. Meanwhile — equipped
With woolly scarf, umbrella, raincoat, gloves,
Stout hiking boots, a torch in hand,
A flask of milky tea next to the eggy sandwiches,
The shiny apple, packed in my knapsack —
I'm going out, and may be gone for some time;
My 'self' — you know the one I mean — has been
Missing in action since 1963, and now the time
Has come to track her down. I'll start with childhood
(Of course), trot through the pre-teens,
Canter sideways to puberty, buck and gallop —
Skirt chasms, circle windmills, ford icy
Streams in spate — through marriage and its
Various dreary ditches (ye Sloughs of Despond).
My legs will tire, my lungs will wheeze, so I'll take
This last appalling year at walking pace, and hope
To pick up traces of my self's most recent
Steps, her lonely trek through winter's landscape.
But when I find her, Doctor, please, your advice:
What to offer the poor lost creature — hug,
Or apple? Hanky? Tea? And will she know me?
Must I coax her, tangle-haired and speechless,

From a tree-house, pull her from a swamp? Drag
Her home by force, and scrub her face? Tame her,
Over years, with music, mirrors, drugs and shiny beads?
Will she hate my work, despise my need to please,
Glaze over when she reads between my lines?
Would I be her shadow, or she, grudgingly, mine?
Might she take over writing duties? Someday, even, edit me?
Will we — now here's the vital question — blend, or bland?
Do let me know, Dee-dubbya — (sincerely, yours, et cetera.)

Don't Look Yet

Hi! My name is Raymond, I'll be your stalker today!
We have no meetings on the schedule; you're due
to avoid me at the market, the office, the snack-bar,
pass me by at the flower stall where I'll be the one
holding a bunch of red carnations; I'll see you home
by bus, keep watch as you burn a batch of spicy fries,
one eye on the TV; peer thru your bathroom window when
you shower and dress for bed (please wear your white
pee-jays, I like them on you best) and while you rest,
I'll nest across the street, in that run-down place for sale,
write confessions in a shaky hand my lawyer's going to call
the best damn evidence of an unbalanced mind he's ever seen.
Between now and then, and between you and me, relax,
try to be patient. I'm stalking just as fast as I can.

Ectoplasmogram

A portrait of John McGlynn

Here he is, the beauteous boy, McGlynn!
Here is the curly haired youth with
A happy chappy face, and a gleam in his eye
(Only the one; the other is kept neatly gleam-free
In case some particular moment calls for shadows,
Despond, coolth). Ecce l'uomo, le voici, eh no?

And he sits here, confidently, at his pectoral peak,
Smoking what might be the twenty thousandth
Of a million glorious cigarettes before he called it
Quits. Thinking — who knows? Thinking something,
Something dark and sharp and bright, but
Beneath that, another level, moodling, curious
About small lives; creatures who hold the secrets of the deep,
The happiness of plankton, coelacanths, starfish, things which
Materialise around him in the dark as shivering ghosts
From other worlds, glowing in the ether, politely asking
For a place by the hearth, for crisps, for beer and sandwiches.

Friend

tucked in my pocket
a charm against sudden chills
arduous tasks
like silk-lined leather gloves
I carry you with me

close enough to whisper
private encouragement for dark days
like a heavy silver earring
I carry you with me

sweetness under the tongue
resilient
dangerously nice
like a big chunk of nougat
I carry you with me

gently reassuring
tactile
a subtle pressure in my chest
like an underwired bra
I carry you with me

the emergency supply
answer to memories of hunger past
like a packet of raisins
I carry you with me

though we never meet again
implacable as time
vital as air
like the moon in the sky
I will carry you with me

Do Great Explorers Really Need an Atlas?

The geography of the moment
Is in the eyes, the curve of lips,
The almost imperceptible movement
Of lines around the mouth, nostrils,
Brows, lashes grazing cheeks.
The earth keeps turning while
Our new world maps are drawn,
Shallows reversed, deeps levelled, peaks razed.
Across lands where once lived only monsters,
Mountains rise, and rivers seek release.
Tectonic platelets shift and re-align at speed
Until, no longer strangers, we're
Close, closer than skin can reach.
Your mouth my cradle,
My time your heartbeat,
My Africa, your New Zealand.

How to Hug

First, please get close. No, no,
closer than that; close enough
to feel the rush of my blood
through skin, shirt, shirt, and skin;
to feel when buttons click and slide
from neck to groin, when seams
meet, as deep human heat travels,
as particles adhere, matter fuses.

Put one arm around my back, where
the ribs rise and fall; the other hand
laid flat against spine; tuck your chin
into my neck, slide ear to ear; there.
Squeeze, gently, until your lungs wheeze,
till knees knock, press in, until the world
slows in its dizzying spin and hold.

And hold.

See?

Now, as I breathe, you breathe,
when my heart slows, yours slows;
when I move, you move too. Eyes
closed, listen to the beat-beat of our
proximity; count to ten, and then
— only if you're ready — let go.

That's how to hug.

'In this gap...'

In this gap, my father, not holding me
In this echo, my mother, not hearing me
In this moment, sister far, brother farther
In this stillness, the lover gone to another
In this emptiness, the ghost children, the lost dog
The rain is where I am, the rain is where they are not

Legerdemain

The right hand knows what
the left hand is doing

the left hand holds a cup,
a hat, a dove, a scarf
where you can see them,
where your eye is drawn
to their shape in motion,
to what they might reveal
as they twist, turn, make
arabesques in the footlights

the left hand is Scheherezade,
imagining tales for you,
conjuring rabbits, coins,
cards, dazzling with speed

and while your gaze is drawn
to that spin of light
the right hand, in a pocket,
holds tight to the seam
of fabric, knuckles white,
hidden from your view

and there, against the
trembling leg, inside the palm,
rests a soul, shyly curled away,
avoiding observation.

Old Man, Outside In

In memory of Leonard Maguire, 1924 - 1977

clothed in a grey-green lichen
of time and wool and beard
holding the smallest roll-up
in the known universe

eyes sparking with dismay
at each encounter with the
powerful nosmo king, whose
rule must be obeyed

addict of the tea leaf, of sugar,
of mustard, peppercorns, chutney,
of potatoes mashed with butter,
of salt — don't forget the salt

skin an ancient map of settlements
defended or abandoned, of tall trees
twisted by siroccos, of nomad-footprints,
of great idea-wells at distant oases

voice powerful as tiger's paws
playing pat-a-cake with mice and thimbles,
the hum of silent engines, brush of bat's wings,
soft-burred, sweet-dark

shy in '30s sailor-suit and buckled shoes,
dreaming infant, eyes full of clouds
stowaway, castaway — a small boy in exile
king of his own lands, journeying home

On Getting no Answer to my e-mail: an Experiment in Thought

Reply, acknowledge, please, receipt
of particles transmitted, those tiny
atoms, sent from me to you in wave
form. Proof of efficacy cannot be observed
with accuracy, nor readings taken, until
arrival's logged, data checked, information
analysed. Reply, please. Are our meters faulty?
Was there no invisible transaction after
all? If one ion of emotion is unequal to
another, it must not attract. Perhaps,
in vacuum, opposites excite, but contact only
creates negativity? Please, reply. I'm sitting here
inside the box, dead/alive, like Schrodinger's cat.

Señor el Cuervo

A crow, at the window, stands
Smoking a twig cigarette, feet
Splayed, black waistcoat fluttering
In the evening heat. 'Hola, amiga!
Por favor, tiene usted un poco de pan?
Jamón? Chorizo?' Turning his beak, his
Bold, bright eye, in query. 'Si, si, señor,
Aquí,' say I, and bring the morsels
On a silver dish. He folds a sandwich,
Carefully, tucks it beneath a wing. 'Gracias,
Gracias. Bien. Tiene un poco de vino?'
I pour *Sangre de Toro,* he dips his head.
'Dulce, sabroso,' snaps his beak. 'Y ahora,
Guapa; vendrá conmigo para bailar?'
I shake off heavy shoes, shed my
Skin, shrug on glossy feathered
Coat and free my wings. Out I hop onto
The ledge, preen, the sky a lilac invitation.
'Aquí estoy, señor — adónde vamos?'
Croaks my new voice. Señor el Cuervo bows.
'Jugar con el viento, chica! Arriba!'

Stupid Shoes

The day I see it,
the moment I voice
my fearful need of
you, you push me away,
gently, and
the planet
tilts

watch
my fingers
slip, one after another
from the lip
of the chasm,
watch the scree
slide under me
towards the
drop

my face is hot
you read my eyes
I cannot look at you
cannot look up.

I leave, instead,
walk home, head down,
cold, heels rubbing
in my stupid shoes,
more skin shed

blind, unbreathing,
crying in the rain,
every painful
step
a syllable
from my own
pathetic
fallacy.

Song of the Siren

I've been sitting here
I've been sitting here waiting
I've been sitting here waiting for you
I've been sitting here waiting for you to pick up the phone.

You'd think
You'd think I'd know
You'd think I'd know by now
You'd think I'd know by now I'm flogging a dead horse.

Are you scared
Are you scared to be seen
Are you scared to be seen with a woman
Are you scared to be seen with a woman with unfettered breasts?

I'm still here
I'm still here in my room
I'm still here in my room listening to the phone ring
I'm still here in my room listening to the phone ring, hunting for a bra.

The Client's Thoughts on Progress

Like a skilled dog-trainer, he
conditions me to respond to
his voice. Already, I will stay,
fetch, stop, sit nicely
on command, eyes alert
to every gesture. I run for him,
bring back sheep, sticks, do tricks.
At silent whistle I come gladly
to heel. Praise sets my tail flying
high, a ribboned flag. I do not growl,
cower, fear the flick of my former
master's heavy hand. Soon,
I'll want to roll at his feet,
have my ears caressed,
tummy rubbed. I will yearn
to lick that kindly bearded face.
Transference, they call it.
A good dog does not bark
or whine, but sometimes
I gnaw this dry scrap, gauge
its familiar texture, cry. The awful
intimacy of being heard, held.
Same bone; new gravy. Love,
in another clever disguise.

'The great car leapt forward...'

In memory of Frances Campbell (1917-2008)

(My mother enjoyed Mary Stewart's romantic thrillers, in one of which
— *Madam, Will You Talk?* — a heroine famously drives a Jaguar up a rough,
icy mountain road, at speed, in the dark.)

Last year was a leap year, and the Aged Campbell
leapt for the last time. Not fearful, in the end,
to soar off the edge of the planet, so many parts
of which she'd conquered by plane, boat, foot,
rendered in watercolours, dwelt in stoically,
(bloody Whetstone, bloody Perth),
driven through, foot down, heroically,
a Boudica of the modern chariot age.

Throughout the Highlands, beloved ancestral grounds,
by roads high and low, wrestling the Ford Consul
firmly through bleak Glen Coe,
by sea to Gibraltar and Spain,
her wartime wonderlands, by sky to Italy,
Tunisia, from film-set to sea-side,
thrilled by ancient Carthage, repro trinkets,
isles flottantes spooned by candle-light.

Happy lone explorer, seasoned globe-trotter,
game for Australia and stations in between,
and always, always talking; emboldened
by social graces learned in dance, Greek-style,
at school, later polished in foxtrots
with firm-chinned chaps of officer rank,
on the Rock, braced by gin & It.

Finally, to France, her chosen heartland,
the last flag on the map, to be
warmed by sunlit days, the camaraderie of
Cordes-sur-Ciel, to be embraced by
les bohèmes, les paysans, les intellectuels,
les ex-pats, tout le monde, enfin —
seventy years on from seeking soulmates in
Hampstead's stuffy *coin — bienvenue chez soi.*

And now, as she'd see it, the chance
to greet old friends — 'I know the face,
I've lost the name, damn, so silly, don't tell me' —
in some celestial café-bar, tobacco-misted. Time
to hug the Aged Pa, (for once, the advance party,
kettle on, night clothes aired), to regale him with
stories about neighbours he'd never met,
or more happily, happenings in their garden.
Romarin, verveine, menthe, keep pushing
through that thick clay soil.

Last year, at the interment, the ground was wet
and hard to open. French graves bore artificial blooms,
plastic *pensées,* granite obelisks, ceramic plaques,
small bronze lines of loss, all too coldly formal
for our liking. This year, that bit of tumbled earth
is smooth, quilted in softest velvet moss,
tucked into the landscape, a natural runway
for newly lightened souls.

The Hero: St George in the 21st Century

The hero talks with dragons
sits right down with them
in their musty hidden caves
toasting marshmallows
on their fiery breath

what do you talk about
i ask him, softly,
health and safety tips,
quick barbecue recipes,
the downsides of arson?

well, life with claws
and without, he replies
scales and skin
tails and wings versus
opposable thumbs

what else, i ask,
hoping for stories of magic
combat, treasure hoards,
enchantment, transformation,
tell me, please, what else?

oh, he smiles, well,
dragonish issues, mainly,
hoarding, swooping, terrorising
the natives, guilt, the usual
relationship problems

are they lonely, then
i ask, like me, and he nods
just as much as anyone can be,
desperately seeking soulmates,
jealousy, anger, loss, depression

and do you heal them
i whisper, when you go to them
do you bind up their wounds
and hold their paws until
they cry, until they feel better?

i try, he says, i can only try —
in the firelight his scars, the ones
i made myself, tugging him here
under my own green wing
look deep, ragged, painful

The Message

We're sending you a message — listen:
Bip bip bip bleeep bip bip bip bleeeep.
Can you hear it, echoing across deep space?
Digital birdsong, bounced from our dead blue star
To your starship, requesting you to plot
A course for orbit. There's land here,
Ready for your survey probes, water
Bubbling under the surface, adequate
Foliage for shelter, forms of animal life
Suited to deep frying. Your crew will like
Our climate, the fizzy hot springs, the gelid
Purple wastes and admirably sharp rocks.
Captain, please land soon, my people
Require carbon-based lifeforms for
Colonisation. It will be painless, even
Mildly euphoric, when we attach our
Suckers to your skins. Truly, in two
Shakes of a comet's tail you will forget
You once were alone in the universe.
Honestly, space worms make good friends.